Reading Plus 2

Clue & Key

CONTENTS

Scope and Sequence

	Title	Topic		Text Type
1	The Enormous Turnip		Gardening	Classic tales
2	Vegetable Gardens	Plant	Vegetables	Nonfiction
3	Sally's Flower Garden		Raising plants	Diary entry
4	Fruit, Fruit, Fruit!		Fruits	Nonfiction
5	Little Red Riding Hood		Hood	Classic tales
6	Teen Clothing Styles	Clothes	Teen fashions	Nonfiction
7	Catching a Clothes Thief		Clothes thieves	Fiction
8	Buying Clothes Online		Online shopping	Nonfiction
9	Stone Soup		Cooking	Classic tales
10	Pots and Pans	Food	Cooking tools	Nonfiction
11	Sara's Cookies		Recipe	Letter
12	A Special Restaurant		Theme restaurant	Nonfiction
13	Anne of Green Gables		School life	Classic tales
14	A Trip to the Museum	School	School field trip	Nonfiction
15	Vote for Me!		School election	Fiction
16	After-School Activities		School activities	Nonfiction

Grammar	Vocabulary
past: regular	enormous, entire, grab, purchase, seed, turnip
during	common, produce, raise, ripen, stalk, vine
prepositions of place	bloom, bud, dig, dirt, hoe, roots
so + be verb + subject	arrive, field, fresh, persimmon, pick, variety
past: irregular	gobble, hood, lie, nightgown, put on, woodcutter
prefer A to B	formal, hole, prefer, resemble, sweatshirt, torn
superlatives: irregular	clue, missing, outfit, sneak, steal, thief
present continuous	convenient, deliver, order, return, sell, try on
but	drop, huge, stir, taste, traveler, village
be able to	equipment, flat, fry, liquid, roast, stew
what + a(n) + adjective + noun !	burn, flour, horrible, ingredient, lump, tray
look like + noun	castle, cheer, customer, feast, knight, unique
want to	adopt, apply for, mistake, orphan, rivalry, scholarship
may	exhibit, focus, fossil, gem, semester, subject
possessive adjectives	clap, collect, election, improve, run, vote
frequency adverbs	activity, join, language, photography, softball, stay

The Enormous Turnip

Before You Read

Read and check.

	True	False
1. Turnips grow in gardens.	☐	☐
2. We cannot eat turnips.	☐	☐
3. Turnips are blue.	☐	☐

New Words 02

Listen and repeat.

1 **turnip:**

2 **seed:**

3 **entire:** whole

4 **grab:** to hold

5 **purchase:** to buy

6 **enormous:** very big

New Sentences

Write a, b, or c.

1 ☐ An old man purchased some seeds.

2 ☐ She grabbed her husband and pulled together.

3 ☐ He saw an enormous turnip in the garden.

The Enormous Turnip

• Topic: Gardening
• Genre: Classic Tales

An old man wanted some turnips, so he purchased some seeds. He planted them and went to sleep. The next day, he looked outside. He saw an enormous turnip in the garden.

"I'm hungry," he said. He went to the garden and tried pulling the turnip up. It didn't move. "Wife, help me," he called. She grabbed her husband and pulled together, but the turnip didn't move. "Son and daughter, help us," they cried together. His children pulled together, but nothing happened. "Dog and cat, help," said the old man. Everyone pulled together, but the turnip stayed in the ground. Finally, a mouse came and helped them. The turnip came out of the ground! They all ate the turnip for an entire week.

Listening Quiz! 04

1 ⓐ Yes   ⓑ No
2 ⓐ the old man   ⓑ the mouse

Details

Choose or write the answer.

1 The old man planted the seeds and went to _____ .

ⓐ garden   ⓑ turnip   ⓒ sleep   ⓓ seeds

2 Everyone pulled together, but the turnip _____ in the ground.

ⓐ stayed   ⓑ planted   ⓒ purchased   ⓓ helped

3 Who was the last one to help the old man?

ⓐ his son   ⓑ his daughter   ⓒ a cat   ⓓ a mouse

4 What did the old man purchase?

- He purchased some _____ .

Main Idea

Choose the main idea.

ⓐ An old man and his family pulled up a big turnip.

ⓑ An old man planted a turnip in his garden.

ⓒ Everyone in the old man's family ate the turnip together.

ⓓ The old man has a son and a daughter.

Organizing

Complete the chart.

Main Character	Event	Result
an _____ man	pulled the _____ up	ate the turnip for a _____

Vocabulary

Fill in the blanks.

> turnip   purchase   enormous   entire   seeds   grab

1. An elephant is the most _____ animal that lives on land.

2. She ate an _____ bag of candy, so she got sick.

3. Do you have enough money to _____ a drink from the store?

4. Please _____ the pen and fill in the blanks.

5. People plant _____ in their gardens in spring.

6. They are having _____ soup for dinner this evening.

Summary 05

Listen to the summary and fill in the blanks.

An old man wanted some _____. So he planted some _____ and grew an

_____ turnip. He tried to _____ it up but couldn't. His _____,

children, and pets helped him. But they couldn't pull it up either. A _____ then

helped, and they succeeded to pull it up.

Tip **One-Minute Grammar!**

Add **ed** or **d** to many verbs to make the past tense. Sometimes, for words like "study," change the **y** to **ied**.

want	⟶	want**ed**
purchase	⟶	purchase**d**
cry	⟶	cr**ied**

Vegetable Gardens

Before You Read

Read and check.

	True	False
1. There are many kinds of vegetables.	☐	☐
2. All vegetables are green.	☐	☐
3. Carrots grow underground.	☐	☐

New Words ◯ 06

Listen and repeat.

❶ **vine:**

❷ **stalk:**

❸ **produce:** to make

❹ **common:** usual

❺ **raise:** to grow

❻ **ripen:** to grow up and be ready to be eaten

New Sentences

Write a, b, or c.

ⓐ 　　ⓑ 　　ⓒ

❶ ☐ Cucumbers grow on vines.

❷ ☐ Gardens can produce lots of vegetables.

❸ ☐ Corn grows high on stalks.

Vegetable Gardens

There are many kinds of vegetables. They come in lots of shapes, sizes, and colors. Some people enjoy raising them in gardens. Cucumbers and beans are often in gardens. They are both green. And they grow on vines. Many gardens have tomatoes and peppers. Both start out green. But when they ripen, they change colors. Tomatoes turn red, yellow, or orange. And peppers may turn red or yellow.

Potatoes are common. They grow under the ground. So do carrots, turnips, and radishes. Corn doesn't grow underground. It grows high in the air on stalks. When it ripens, it turns bright yellow. During summer, gardens can produce lots of vegetables. They have many colors. And they are all delicious and good for your health!

Listening Quiz! 08
1 ⓐ Yes   ⓑ No
2 ⓐ red   ⓑ yellow

Details

Choose or write the answer.

1 _____ turn red, yellow, or orange.

ⓐ Tomatoes   ⓑ Beans   ⓒ Radishes   ⓓ Potatoes

2 Corn grows high in the _____ on stalks.

ⓐ vines   ⓑ underground   ⓒ air   ⓓ color

3 Where do cucumbers grow?

ⓐ on stalks   ⓑ on vines   ⓒ on trees   ⓓ underground

4 What plants grow underground?

- Potatoes, carrots, turnips, and _____ grow underground.

Main Idea

Choose the main idea.

ⓐ Vegetables are good to eat.

ⓑ Both cucumbers and beans grow on vines.

ⓒ Corn turns yellow when it ripens.

ⓓ There are many kinds of vegetables.

Organizing

Complete the chart.

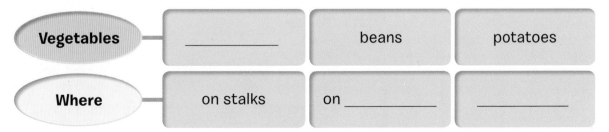

| Vegetables | _____ | beans | potatoes |
| Where | on stalks | on _____ | _____ |

Vocabulary

Fill in the blanks.

> vine   common   ripen   stalk   raise   produce

1 There was a lot of corn growing on the _____ .

2 The company will _____ many different cars.

3 The _____ is growing up the side of the building.

4 The apples will _____ in fall.

5 They _____ chickens and pigs on their farm.

6 One _____ food people eat a lot of is rice.

Summary

Listen to the summary and fill in the blanks.

People _____ many kinds of _____ in their gardens. _____ and

beans are green and grow on vines. Tomatoes and _____ change colors when

they _____. Potatoes and other vegetables grow underground. Corn grows

high on stalks. Many vegetables look different, but they all taste _____!

🔔 Tip One-Minute Grammar!

Use **during** to talk about something that happens in a period of time.

During summer, gardens can produce lots of vegetables.

It often snows **during** the winter.

Sally's Flower Garden

Before You Read

Read and check.

	True	False
1. A tomato is a flower.	☐	☐
2. Flowers need water to live.	☐	☐
3. All flowers are the same color.	☐	☐

New Words 🔊 10

Listen and repeat.

❶ **hoe:**

❷ **roots:**

❸ **bud:**

❹ **bloom:** to open into a flower

❺ **dirt:** ground

❻ **dig:** to make a hole in the ground

New Sentences

Write a, b, or c.

ⓐ 　　ⓑ 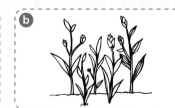　　ⓒ

❶ ☐ Some of the plants are getting buds.

❷ ☐ I got a hoe and dug up the dirt.

❸ ☐ They bloom and have beautiful flowers.

Sally's Flower Garden

• Topic: Raising Plants
• Genre: Diary Entry

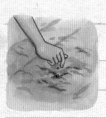

Dear Diary,

I'm very excited. Three weeks ago, I started a flower garden in my backyard. I got a hoe and dug up the dirt. Then I planted some seeds in the ground. I watered them every day to give them strong roots.

Two weeks ago, they started coming up above the ground. At first, they were as small as my little finger. But now my flowers are getting bigger. Some of them are getting buds. Soon, they will bloom and have beautiful flowers. Oh, what flowers did I plant? I planted some irises. And I also have violets and carnations, too. They will have many different colors. And I have one sunflower. It will grow as high as a small tree.

Sally

Listening Quiz! ● 12

1 ⓐ Yes   ⓑ No

2 ⓐ last week
ⓑ three weeks ago

Details

Choose or write the answer.

1 Sally got a _____ and dug up the dirt.

    ⓐ hoe   ⓑ rake   ⓒ shovel   ⓓ spade

2 Now the flowers are getting _____.

    ⓐ stronger   ⓑ bigger   ⓒ prettier   ⓓ shorter

3 What will the flowers do soon?

    ⓐ dig   ⓑ ripen   ⓒ die   ⓓ bloom

4 What flowers did Sally plant?

    - She planted irises, violets, carnations, and one _____.

Main Idea

Choose the main idea.

    ⓐ Sally's flowers have already started to bloom.

    ⓑ Sally planted some flowers, and now they are growing.

    ⓒ Sally has a sunflower that is as high as a small tree.

    ⓓ Sally watered her flowers every day.

Organizing

Complete the chart.

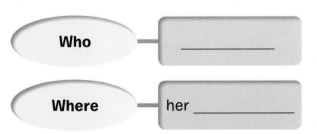

Who _____

Where her _____

What she did
- dug up the _____
- _____ some seeds
- watered them every day

Vocabulary

Fill in the blanks.

hoe	dig	dirt	roots	bud	bloom

1 Do you know when the flowers are going to _____ ?

2 The tree's _____ are very deep in the ground.

3 I can see a _____ on that plant. It will become a flower soon.

4 Get a _____ . We have to dig up these weeds.

5 Take your shoes off right now! You're bringing _____ into the house.

6 A person with a shovel can _____ very quickly.

Summary 13

Listen to the summary and fill in the blanks.

Sally wanted a flower _____. So she dug up some dirt with a _____ and

planted some _____. She _____ the plants every day. Then they started

to grow. Now, her plants have some _____. They will _____ soon. She

has irises, violets, carnations, and even a sunflower.

🖑 **One-Minute Grammar!**

Use prepositions like **in**, **above**, **on**, and **below** to describe the place of different objects.

I started a flower garden **in** my backyard.
The roots are **below** the ground.

Fruit, Fruit, Fruit!

Before You Read

Read and check.

	True	False
1. Oranges and lemons are fruits.	☐	☐
2. Strawberries grow in the winter.	☐	☐
3. Blueberries and blackberries are berries.	☐	☐

New Words 🔊 14

Listen and repeat.

1 persimmon:

2 pick:

3 field:

4 fresh: new

5 arrive: to come

6 variety: a kind

New Sentences

Write a, b, or c.

a	b	c

1 ☐ There are many varieties of fruits.

2 ☐ In spring, grapefruits are fresh.

3 ☐ Apples are very popular fruits when fall arrives.

Fruit, Fruit, Fruit!

There are many varieties of fruits. In many countries, fruits grow at different times of the year. So people can enjoy different fruits all year long.

In spring, strawberries and grapefruits are fresh. People enjoy eating strawberries as they pick them in the fields. When summer comes, there are many other fruits. Cherries, peaches, plums, and apricots are ripe in summer. So are many berries. Some are blueberries, raspberries, and blackberries. Melons ripen in the summer and fall. And apples are very popular fruits when fall arrives. So are persimmons. Grapes and pears are ripe in this season, too. In winter, it is cold. So many fruits can't grow. But citrus fruits like oranges and lemons are ripe then.

Listening Quiz! ● 16

1 ⓐ Yes   ⓑ No
2 ⓐ orange   ⓑ strawberry

Details

Choose or write the answer.

1 In spring, strawberries and grapefruits are _____.

ⓐ popular　　ⓑ fresh　　ⓒ different　　ⓓ old

2 Melons _____ in the summer and fall.

ⓐ pick　　ⓑ grow　　ⓒ ripen　　ⓓ arrive

3 What kind of fruits is very popular in fall?

ⓐ citrus fruits　　ⓑ berries　　ⓒ melons　　ⓓ apples

4 Why cannot many fruits grow in winter?

- Because it is _____ in winter.

Main Idea

Choose the main idea.

ⓐ The most delicious fruits grow in the summer.

ⓑ Apples and grapes are ripe in the fall.

ⓒ Some people love to eat lots of fruit.

ⓓ Different kinds of fruits grow in each season.

Organizing

Complete the chart.

Spring	_____	_____	Winter
_____ grapefruits	berries peaches plums	pears apples persimmons	_____ lemons

Vocabulary

Fill in the blanks.

> variety　　fresh　　pick　　field　　arrive　　persimmon

1 We love to ＿＿＿＿＿ strawberries in the field and eat them.

2 What time will your train ＿＿＿＿＿ at the station?

3 I always drink ＿＿＿＿＿ orange juice in the morning.

4 The ＿＿＿＿＿ on the tree looks like it is ripe.

5 She has a ＿＿＿＿＿ of pens and pencils in her bag.

6 Let's go to the ＿＿＿＿＿ and throw the ball around.

Summary 17

Listen to the summary and fill in the blanks.

There is a variety of ＿＿＿＿＿＿＿ all year long. In spring, grapefruits and strawberries

are fresh. In summer, people can ＿＿＿＿＿＿ peaches and ＿＿＿＿＿＿. Many berries

are ripe in summer, too. In fall, apples are ＿＿＿＿＿＿. So are grapes, ＿＿＿＿＿＿,

and pears. When winter ＿＿＿＿＿＿, there are few fruits.

Tip **One-Minute Grammar!**

Use **so+be verb+subject** to show how one thing is similar to something else mentioned in an earlier sentence.

Cherries are ripe in summer. **So are berries**.
Apples are very popular fruits. **So are persimmons**.

Little Red Riding Hood

Before You Read

Read and check.

	True	False
1. A hood is a part of pants.	☐	☐
2. Children often love their grandmothers.	☐	☐
3. Wolves can speak in real world.	☐	☐

New Words 18

Listen and repeat.

❶ **woodcutter:**

❷ **nightgown:**

❸ **hood:**

❹ **lie:** to be flat in bed

❺ **put on:** to wear

❻ **gobble:** to eat very fast

New Sentences

Write a, b, or c.

 ⓐ

 ⓑ

 ⓒ

❶ ☐ The wolf lay in bed.

❷ ☐ The girl loved the hood.

❸ ☐ The wolf put on her nightgown.

Little Red Riding Hood

• Topic: Hood
• Genre: Classic Tales

There was once a little girl whom everyone loved. Her grandmother especially loved her. She gave her granddaughter a riding hood of red velvet. The girl loved the hood, so she always wore it. Soon, people called her "Little Red Riding Hood."

One day, her grandmother got sick. So she put on her coat and boots. Then she left home. But a wolf went to her grandmother's house. He ate the grandmother, put on her nightgown, and lay in bed. Soon, Little Red Riding Hood arrived.

"Grandma, you look strange," she said. "That's because I'm a wolf!" the wolf said, and he gobbled her up. Then, a woodcutter came by. He cut the wolf open, and out came Little Red Riding Hood and her grandmother!

Listening Quiz! ● 20

1 ⓐ Yes   ⓑ No

2 ⓐ a nightgown   ⓑ a hood

Details

Choose or write the answer.

1 Little Red Riding Hood always wore the _____ .
ⓐ skirt   ⓑ nightgown   ⓒ boots   ⓓ hood

2 "Grandma, you look _____ ," she said.
ⓐ strange   ⓑ hungry   ⓒ old   ⓓ funny

3 What was the girl's hood made of?
ⓐ silk   ⓑ velvet   ⓒ cotton   ⓓ wool

4 Why did Little Red Riding Hood go to her grandmother's house?
- Because her grandmother got _____ .

Main Idea

Choose the main idea.

ⓐ Little Red Riding Hood had a red velvet hood.

ⓑ A woodcutter saved Little Red Riding Hood and her grandmother.

ⓒ A woodcutter chased a wolf away from Little Red Riding Hood.

ⓓ Wolves are dangerous animals and sometimes attack people.

Organizing

Complete the chart.

A _____ went to the grandmother's house and ate the grandmother.

When Little Red Riding Hood arrived, the wolf _____ her up.

A _____ cut the wolf open and saved both of them.

Vocabulary

Fill in the blanks.

> hood   put on   nightgown   lie   gobble   woodcutter

 His _____ keeps him dry when it rains.

② Some dogs _____ their food very quickly.

③ The _____ is going to cut some trees down.

④ _____ down in the bed and go to sleep.

⑤ Hurry up and _____ your clothes!

⑥ My mother wears a _____ when she goes to bed.

Summary 🔘21

Listen to the summary and fill in the blanks.

Little Red Riding Hood loved her _____ and always wore it. One day, she

went to her grandmother's house. But a wolf got there first, _____ the

grandmother, and put on her _____. Then Little Red Riding Hood _____.

The wolf _____ her up. Then a _____ killed the wolf and saved them.

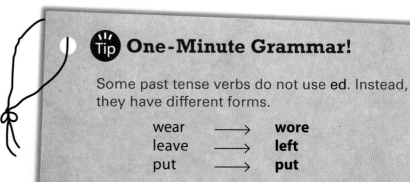

Tip 🔔 One-Minute Grammar!

Some past tense verbs do not use ed. Instead, they have different forms.

wear	⟶	**wore**
leave	⟶	**left**
put	⟶	**put**

Teen Clothing Styles

Before You Read

Read and check.

	True	False
1. Teens often wear casual clothes.	☐	☐
2. There are many clothing styles.	☐	☐
3. Parents always wear hoodies to work.	☐	☐

New Words 22

Listen and repeat.

1 **hole:**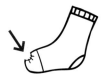

2 **formal:** not casual

3 **prefer:** to like

4 **resemble:** to look like

5 **torn:** pulled apart

6 **sweatshirt:** a heavy, long-sleeved T-shirt

New Sentences

Write a, b, or c.

 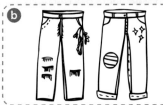 

1 ☐ Some people like formal clothes.

2 ☐ The jeans have holes in them.

3 ☐ She prefers casual clothes to formal clothes.

Teen Clothing Styles

There are many types of clothing styles. Everyone has his or her own style. Some people like formal clothes. Others prefer different kinds of clothes. Many teenagers have their own style, too.

Teenagers like to look different from other people. They don't want to resemble their parents. They often prefer casual clothes to formal clothes. Many teens wear T-shirts and blue jeans. Sometimes, the jeans have holes in them. So people call them torn blue jeans. Some teens love wearing sweatshirts and sweatpants. They especially love hoodies. These are sweatshirts with hoods. However, their parents really dislike hoodies. They want their children to wear nicer-looking clothes. But teenagers don't want to do this. They prefer having their own style.

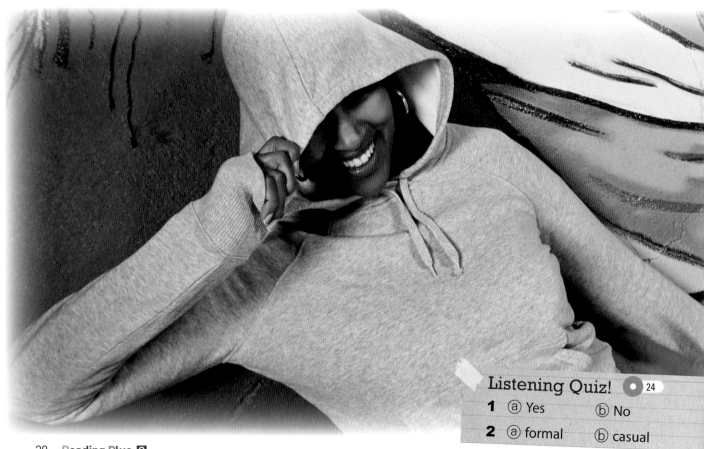

Listening Quiz! 24

1 ⓐ Yes   ⓑ No

2 ⓐ formal   ⓑ casual

Details

Choose or write the answer.

1 Teens often prefer casual clothes to _____ clothes.

ⓐ jeans   ⓑ sweatshirts   ⓒ torn   ⓓ formal

2 However, teens' parents really _____ hoodies.

ⓐ resemble   ⓑ dislike   ⓒ prefer   ⓓ wear

3 Who do teens often not want to resemble?

ⓐ their teachers   ⓑ their brothers and sisters   ⓒ their friends   ⓓ their parents

4 What do people call jeans with holes in them?

- People call them _____ _____ _____.

Main Idea

Choose the main idea.

ⓐ A lot of teens love to wear hoodies.

ⓑ Parents don't like the clothes that teens wear.

ⓒ Many teens prefer to wear casual clothes.

ⓓ Some teenagers wear T-shirts and blue jeans.

Organizing

Complete the chart.

Teen Clothing Styles

- T-shirts and _____
- _____ and sweatpants
- sweatshirts with hoods: _____

Vocabulary

Fill in the blanks.

> sweatshirt   resemble   formal   hole   prefer   torn

1 I think that I _____ my mother a lot.

2 It's cool, so wear a _____ outside today.

3 There is a _____ in the wall.

4 My shirt got _____ when I tried to jump over the fence.

5 Do you _____ action movies to comedies?

6 Lisa's father always wears _____ clothes to work.

Summary 25

Listen to the summary and fill in the blanks.

Everyone has his or her own clothing _____. Teenagers like to look different

from others. They _____ casual clothes to _____ clothes. They often

wear T-shirts and blue jeans with _____. Some _____ really love

sweatshirts and sweatpants. They even _____ hoodies sometimes.

Tip One-Minute Grammar!

Use **prefer A to B** to describe how you like something more than another thing.

They **prefer** casual clothes **to** formal clothes.
She **prefers** T-shirts **to** blouses.

Unit 07

Catching a Clothes Thief

Before You Read

Read and check.

	True	False
1. Department stores sell clothes.	☐	☐
2. The police never catch thieves.	☐	☐
3. There are price tags on new clothes.	☐	☐

New Words 🔊 26

Listen and repeat.

1 **thief:**

2 **missing:** gone

3 **clue:** a hint

4 **outfit:** clothes

5 **sneak:** to move quietly

6 **steal:** to take something without paying for it

New Sentences

Write a, b, or c.

a    b    c

1 ☐ The police looked around for clues.

2 ☐ A thief sneaked into the store.

3 ☐ Some clothes were missing.

Catching a Clothes Thief

- Topic: Clothes Thieves
- Genre: Fiction

The department store was closed. But, suddenly, one of the doors opened. A thief sneaked into the store. He walked all around the store. He looked at many different clothes. He saw suits, pants, shirts, and neckties. He grabbed many clothes and put them in a bag. He didn't steal any cheap outfits. He only took the most expensive items.

The next day, the workers arrived. They found some clothes were missing. So they called the police. The police looked around for clues, but there weren't any. Just then, a very well-dressed man walked into the store. Beep beep beep! The alarm went off. The police grabbed the man. It was the thief! He had forgotten to take the price tags off the clothes!

Listening Quiz! 28

1 ⓐ Yes   ⓑ No
2 ⓐ to a supermarket
   ⓑ to a department store

Choose or write the answer.

1 The thief only took the _____ items.

ⓐ most stylish ⓑ cheapest ⓒ most expensive ⓓ prettiest

2 The police _____ around for clues.

ⓐ ran ⓑ walked ⓒ looked ⓓ saw

3 Who found that some clothes were missing?

ⓐ the workers ⓑ the well-dressed man ⓒ the police ⓓ the thief

4 What had the thief forgotten?

- He had forgotten to take the price _____ off the clothes.

Main Idea

Choose the main idea.

ⓐ A thief stole some clothes from a department store.

ⓑ The police couldn't find any clues about the thief.

ⓒ The store alarm went off when the thief came in.

ⓓ A thief robbed a store, but the police caught him.

Organizing

Complete the chart.

Main Character	Event	Result
a _____	stole _____ outfits	got caught by the _____

Fill in the blanks.

| thief | sneak | steal | outfit | missing | clue |

1 I need a _____ to find the hidden treasure.

2 You shouldn't _____ things! Always pay for them.

3 Don't try to _____ away. Stay here and clean up this mess.

4 My bag is _____ ! I can't find it anywhere.

5 The _____ stole some money from the bank.

6 What kind of _____ are you wearing to dinner tonight?

Summary ⦿ 29

Listen to the summary and fill in the blanks.

A thief _____ into a department store. He wanted to _____ many

expensive _____. The next day, the police came. They couldn't find any

_____. Then a man walked into the store. The _____ went off. It was the

thief! He never took the tags off the stolen _____.

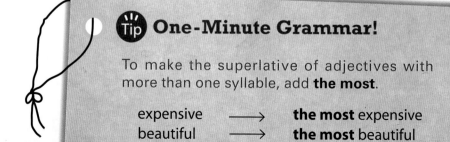

Tip **One-Minute Grammar!**

To make the superlative of adjectives with more than one syllable, add **the most**.

expensive ⟶ **the most** expensive
beautiful ⟶ **the most** beautiful

Buying Clothes Online

Before You Read

Read and check.

	True	False
1. Clothing stores sell food.	☐	☐
2. People can buy clothes on the Internet.	☐	☐
3. People can visit online stores in person.	☐	☐

New Words 🔊 30

Listen and repeat.

1 **try on:**

2 **return:** to take back

3 **deliver:** to take to another place

4 **convenient:** easy and comfortable

5 **sell:** to give something in exchange for money

6 **order:** to ask for something in a shop or restaurant

New Sentences

Write a, b, or c.

1 ☐ The clothes will be delivered to their homes.

2 ☐ People can't try on the clothes.

3 ☐ She orders it by clicking her mouse on the item.

Buying Clothes Online

Do you know there are some stores that never close and sell their clothes for 24 hours? Yes, they are on the Internet. People are often busy. So they don't have time to shop. With online clothing stores, they can do their shopping from home. They just go to the company's website. Then they find clothes they like and order them by clicking their mouse on the item. The clothes will be delivered to their homes. It is easy and convenient.

But online shopping isn't perfect. People can't try on the clothes. So they may buy the wrong sizes. The real clothes often look different from the ones on the website. And returning clothes is inconvenient, too. Still, many people are buying clothes online these days.

Listening Quiz! 32

1 ⓐ Yes   ⓑ No

2 ⓐ home   ⓑ school

Choose or write the answer.

1 Online stores never close and _____ their clothes for 24 hours.
ⓐ sell   ⓑ click   ⓒ buy   ⓓ order

2 People may buy the wrong _____ when they shop online
ⓐ prices   ⓑ styles   ⓒ sizes   ⓓ colors

3 What is inconvenient to do with online clothing stores?
ⓐ buy clothes   ⓑ return clothes   ⓒ order clothes   ⓓ look at clothes

4 Why do people like ordering from online clothing stores?
- It is easy and _____.

Main Idea

Choose the main idea.

ⓐ There are many online clothing stores these days.
ⓑ Buying clothes online has good points and bad points.
ⓒ You can't try on clothes, and returning clothes is inconvenient, too.
ⓓ Many people don't have time to shop at stores.

Organizing

Complete the chart.

Good Points of Online Shopping	Bad Points of Online Shopping
• can do shopping from _____ • clothes will be delivered • _____ and convenient	• can't try on clothes • may buy _____ sizes • _____ clothes is inconvenient

Fill in the blanks.

> sells order deliver convenient try on return

1. The store _____ drink and snacks.

2. You should _____ that shirt before you buy it.

3. The post office will _____ your package in one hour.

4. If you don't like the video game, _____ it and get another one.

5. What would you like to _____ for dinner?

6. Taking the bus to school is really _____ .

Summary 33

Listen to the summary and fill in the blanks.

There are many clothing stores, but now people are buying clothes _____. They

check the company's _____. They _____ the clothes, and the company

_____ them. It's very convenient. But they can't try on clothes, so they may

get the wrong _____. And returning clothes is _____, too.

Tip One-Minute Grammar!

Use the present continuous tense to talk about something you are doing now.
be + verb -ing

People **are buying** clothes online.
I **am watching** television right now.

Stone Soup

Before You Read

Read and check.

	True	False
1. People can eat stones.	☐	☐
2. You need water to make soup.	☐	☐
3. You make soup in a pot.	☐	☐

New Words 34

Listen and repeat.

1 **stir**:

2 **taste**: to try or test the flavor

3 **huge**: very big

4 **village**: a very small town

5 **drop**: to let something fall down

6 **traveler**: a person who is taking a trip

New Sentences

Write a, b, or c.

1 ☐ He tasted the soup.

2 ☐ He dropped a big stone in the pot.

3 ☐ He put a huge pot of water over the fire.

Stone Soup

Three travelers visited a village. They were hungry, but no one gave them any food. The oldest traveler started a fire and put a huge pot of water over it. Then he dropped a big stone in it. "What are you making?" asked a villager. "Stone soup," he answered.

"Stone soup? What's that?" he asked. "It's delicious, but it needs carrots to have a better flavor," the traveler said. The villager ran to his house and brought some carrots back. The traveler stirred the soup and tasted it. "Not bad, but it could use some potatoes," he said. Another villager put in some potatoes. Soon, every villager put something in the soup. "This is the most delicious soup ever," said someone. The soup was enjoyed by all.

Listening Quiz! ● 36
1 ⓐ Yes ⓑ No
2 ⓐ a villager ⓑ a traveler

Details

Choose or write the answer.

1 Three travelers visited a _____.

ⓐ city   ⓑ village   ⓒ town   ⓓ farm

2 The oldest traveler started a fire and put a huge _____ of water over it.

ⓐ potato   ⓑ pot   ⓒ stone   ⓓ carrot

3 Where did the traveler put the stone?

ⓐ in the fire   ⓑ in the village   ⓒ in the pot   ⓓ in the house

4 What did the villagers add to the soup?

- They added _____, potatoes, and something others.

Main Idea

Choose the main idea.

ⓐ The villagers didn't give the travelers any food.

ⓑ No one can make a soup with just a stone in it.

ⓒ Some travelers tricked a village into giving them some food.

ⓓ The villagers added carrots and potatoes to the soup.

Organizing

Complete the chart.

Main Characters	Place	Events
three _____	a _____	made stone _____

Vocabulary

Fill in the blanks.

> traveler village huge drop taste stir

1. A whale is a _____ animal that lives in the sea.

2. Don't _____ the glass, or it will break.

3. That _____ has visited many foreign countries during his life.

4. I have to _____ the soup until it begins to boil.

5. Will you _____ the chicken and see if it is done?

6. Only a few people actually lived in the tiny _____.

Summary 37

Listen to the summary and fill in the blanks.

Three travelers visited a _____. They were _____, but no one gave

them any food. One traveler started _____ a stone in a _____ pot. He

said he was making _____ soup. The villagers started to _____ carrots,

potatoes, and other food in the pot. Then everyone ate the soup.

Tip One-Minute Grammar!

Use **but** to connect two sentences. The sentences usually have opposite or different meanings.

They were hungry. + No one gave them any food.
→ They were hungry, **but** no one gave them any food.

Pots and Pans

Before You Read

Read and check.

	True	False
1. People cook with pots and pans.	☐	☐
2. People can fry eggs on pans.	☐	☐
3. A pancake is a cooking tool.	☐	☐

New Words 🔊 38

Listen and repeat.

1 fry:

2 flat:

3 equipment: tools

4 stew: a thick soup

5 liquid: a fluid like water or juice

6 roast: to cook food in an oven

New Sentences

Write a, b, or c.

a	b	c

1 ☐ A cook makes stew in a pot.

2 ☐ A griddle is a flat pan.

3 ☐ A cook roasts a chicken in the oven.

Pots and Pans

Every cook needs some equipment in the kitchen. So, most of them have many pots and pans. Without them, they wouldn't be able to cook.

Some cooks like having big pots. They make stew and soup in them. And they also cook pasta like spaghetti in them. These pots can hold lots of water and other liquids. Cooks use smaller pots for making sauces.

Cooks always have many kinds of pans, too. They especially need frying pans. They are able to fry eggs, hamburgers, and other kinds of food on them. Roasting pans are helpful, too. Cooks put chickens or hams on them and then roast them in the oven. Finally, most cooks have a griddle. It's a flat pan perfect for making pancakes!

Listening Quiz! 40

1 ⓐ Yes   ⓑ No

2 ⓐ a pot   ⓑ a pan

Details

Choose or write the answer.

1 Cooks use smaller pots for making _____.

ⓐ chicken   ⓑ sauces   ⓒ spaghetti   ⓓ pancakes

2 Every cook needs some equipment in the _____.

ⓐ bedroom   ⓑ bathroom   ⓒ living room   ⓓ kitchen

3 Where do cooks often put roasting pans?

ⓐ in the oven   ⓑ on the stove   ⓒ on a griddle   ⓓ in a pot

4 What do cooks make in big pots?

- They make _____ , soup, and pasta in them.

Main Idea

Choose the main idea.

ⓐ Some cooks make spaghetti in big pots.

ⓑ A good cook should have some pans in the kitchen.

ⓒ Cooks put roasting pans in the oven.

ⓓ Cooks use many different kinds of pots and pans.

Organizing

Complete the chart.

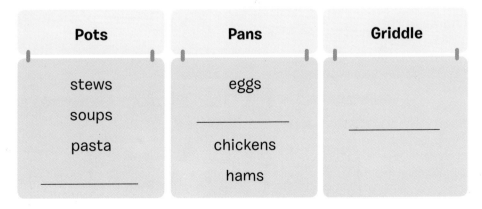

Pots	Pans	Griddle
stews	eggs	
soups	_____	_____
pasta	chickens	
_____	hams	

Vocabulary

Fill in the blanks.

flat   stew   liquid   fry   roast   equipment

1 Many people like to eat _____ during the winter.

2 Her mother will _____ some meat in the oven for dinner.

3 The repairman has a lot of _____ in his toolbox.

4 The area is very _____ with no mountains or hills.

5 Water is a _____, and so are orange juice and soda.

6 I always _____ two eggs for breakfast in the morning.

Summary 41

Listen to the summary and fill in the blanks.

Cooks have _____ like pots and pans for their kitchens. Pots are big and can

hold lots of _____. Cooks make stew, soup, and _____ with them. Cooks

use frying pans to _____ eggs and other foods. They can also _____

chickens and hams in the _____.

Tip One-Minute Grammar!

Use **be able to** to describe an ability. It often has the same meaning as can.

They **are able to** fry eggs.
He **is able to** run fast.

Unit 11

Sara's Cookies

Read and check.

	True	False
1. Cookies taste sweet.	☐	☐
2. The color of flour is green.	☐	☐
3. We need some eggs to make cookies.	☐	☐

New Words 🔊 42

Listen and repeat.

1 tray:

2 flour: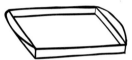

3 lump: a piece

4 burn: to be on fire

5 horrible: very bad

6 ingredient: something needed to make food

New Sentences

Write a, b, or c.

 a

 b

 c

1 ☐ I smelled something burning.

2 ☐ I got all the ingredients.

3 ☐ I put lumps of cookie dough on a tray.

Sara's Cookies

- Topic: Recipe
- Genre: Letter

Dear Lisa,

I tried making some cookies yesterday. You won't believe what happened. First, I got all the ingredients. I needed flour, sugar, eggs, butter and chocolate chips. I mixed everything together. It looked really good. Then I heated the oven. I put lumps of cookie dough on a tray. And then I put it in the oven.

But guess what happened next? My friend Amy called me. We talked for twenty minutes. Then I smelled something burning. It was the cookies! They looked horrible! Then my mother came home. She went to the kitchen and looked at me and my cookies. And then she said, "Let's go to the store and buy some cookies." What a great mom!

Your friend, Sara

Listening Quiz! 44

1 ⓐ Yes   ⓑ No

2 ⓐ Sara   ⓑ Lisa

Choose or write the answer.

1 Sara mixed everything together, and then she heated the _____.

ⓐ cookies ⓑ chocolate chips ⓒ oven ⓓ bowl

2 She smelled the cookies _____.

ⓐ mixing ⓑ baking ⓒ heating ⓓ burning

3 Who wrote the letter?

ⓐ Lisa ⓑ Amy ⓒ Sara ⓓ Sara's mother

4 What ingredients did she need to make the cookies?

- She needed flour, _____, eggs, butter, and chocolate chips.

Main Idea

Choose the main idea.

ⓐ Sara tried to make some cookies, but she burned them.

ⓑ Sara and her mother bought some cookies at the store.

ⓒ Sara talked on the telephone with her friend Amy.

ⓓ Sara needed many ingredients to make the cookies.

Organizing

Complete the chart.

Sara prepared all of the _____ to make cookies.

↓

She put the cookie tray in the _____ and started baking them.

↓

She cooked them for too long and _____ the cookies.

Fill in the blanks.

> flour   ingredient   lump   tray   burn   horrible

1 _____ is as white as snow.

2 She put a _____ of mashed potatoes on her plate.

3 This tastes _____. You put too much salt on the food.

4 I need one more _____ before I can start making the cookies.

5 My mother put some cups on a _____ and brought them to us.

6 If you touch that hot stove, you are going to _____ your hand.

Summary 45

Listen to the summary and fill in the blanks.

Sara prepared the ingredients for _____. She mixed them together and made

_____ of dough. She put them in the oven and baked them. But she cooked

them for twenty _____. So they started _____. They tasted _____.

So Sara and her mother went to the _____ for some cookies.

Tip **One-Minute Grammar!**

Use **What a(n) + adjective + noun!** to make an exclamation about something. Use this when you feel a strong emotion about something.

What a great mom!
What an old car!

A Special Restaurant

Before You Read

Read and check.

	True	False
1. All restaurants look the same.	☐	☐
2. Some restaurants have entertainment.	☐	☐
3. A knight can ride a horse.	☐	☐

New Words 🔊 46

Listen and repeat.

1 **knight:**

2 **castle:**

3 **cheer:**

4 **feast:** a big dinner

5 **unique:** very special

6 **customer:** a person who buys goods or services

New Sentences

Write a, b, or c.

ⓐ  ⓑ  ⓒ

1 ☐ The knights ride horses.

2 ☐ It looks like a castle!

3 ☐ They eat a delicious feast of meat and vegetables.

A Special Restaurant

As you walk down the stairs, you can see the gothic dining room. Now, you are back in the 15th century!

Theme restaurants make dining a unique experience. One of them is Medieval Times. It doesn't look like a restaurant. It looks like a castle! Diners go back to the Middle Ages at this place. They get to eat a delicious feast of meat and vegetables. But that's not the best part.

There is a show at the restaurant. There are six knights in the show. Every diner cheers for the knights. The knights ride horses. They fight each other for over two hours. So customers get a wonderful meal and entertainment during their night out.

Listening Quiz! 48

1 ⓐ Yes   ⓑ No

2 ⓐ a castle   ⓑ a house

Details

Choose or write the answer.

1 Theme restaurants make dining a _____ experience.

ⓐ unique   ⓑ expensive   ⓒ boring   ⓓ delicious

2 There are six _____ in the show.

ⓐ feasts   ⓑ castles   ⓒ customers   ⓓ knights

3 What do the diners eat at the restaurant?

ⓐ a feast   ⓑ fruit   ⓒ seafood   ⓓ nothing

4 What do the knights do in the show?

- The knights ride horses and _____ each other.

Main Idea

Choose the main idea.

ⓐ The knights at Medieval Times fight each other.

ⓑ Medieval Times is a theme restaurant that serves meals and enterainment.

ⓒ People in the Middle Ages lived in big castles.

ⓓ The show at Medieval Times lasts for two hours.

Organizing

Complete the chart.

_____ restaurant

Medieval Times

six _____ in a show

looks like a _____

a feast of meat and _____

Vocabulary

Fill in the blanks.

> customer   unique   castle   feast   knight   cheer

1 The king and the queen lived in a big _____ on top of a hill.

2 We are going to _____ for our team at the baseball game.

3 We always have a big _____ on Thanksgiving.

4 The _____ is wearing armor and riding on a horse.

5 The _____ was unhappy with the service at the store.

6 This painting is _____. There is not another one like it anywhere.

Summary 49

Listen to the summary and fill in the blanks.

Some _____ offer their customers a _____ experience. Medieval Times

is a restaurant that looks like a _____. The diners there eat a huge _____.

They also get to watch a _____. There are six knights. The knights fight for two

hours. And the customers _____ for them.

Tip **One-Minute Grammar!**

Use **look like** to describe how something looks. You should use a noun after this expression.

The restaurant **looks like** a castle.
The meal **looks like** a feast.

Anne of Green Gables

Before You Read

Read and check.

	True	False
1. All children live with their parents.	☐	☐
2. People can die of a heart attack.	☐	☐
3. A gable is a top part of a building.	☐	☐

New Words 50

Listen and repeat.

1 **mistake**: an error

2 **adopt**: to take as one's child

3 **orphan**: a child with no parents

4 **apply for**: to try to get

5 **scholarship**: money for school

6 **rivalry**: a competition with another person

New Sentences

Write a, b, or c.

1 ☐ Anne has a rivalry with Gilbert.

2 ☐ Anne makes many mistakes.

3 ☐ She applies for a scholarship.

Anne of Green Gables

• Topic: School Life
• Genre: Classic Tales

Matthew and Marilla live on a farm called Green Gables. They want to adopt an orphan boy to help on the farm. But the orphanage wrongly sends a girl, Anne.

At first, Anne makes many mistakes. But she still tries very hard. At school, she makes a friendship with Diana but has a rivalry with Gilbert. As Anne grows up, she becomes an excellent student. She applies for a scholarship to a university, and she gets it. However, Matthew suddenly dies of a heart attack. And Marilla has some health problems. Anne decides to stay home. Gilbert gives his teaching job to Anne. So she can stay close to home and care for Marilla. After Gilbert does this, he and Anne become close friends.

Listening Quiz! 52

1 ⓐ Yes   ⓑ No
2 ⓐ a good student
        ⓑ a bad student

Details

Choose or write the answer.

1 Matthew and Marilla live on a _____ called Green Gables.

    ⓐ school   ⓑ farm   ⓒ orphanage   ⓓ house

2 Matthew and Marilla want to _____ an orphan boy.

    ⓐ make   ⓑ help   ⓒ decide   ⓓ adopt

3 Who does Anne have a rivalry with?

    ⓐ Diana   ⓑ Matthew   ⓒ Marilla   ⓓ Gilbert

4 What happens to Matthew?

    - He dies of a _____ _____ .

Main Idea

Choose the main idea.

    ⓐ Anne has a busy life growing up on Green Gables.

    ⓑ Anne gets adopted from the orphanage.

    ⓒ Anne and Gilbert have a rivalry with each other.

    ⓓ Anne takes care of Marilla after Matthew dies.

Organizing

Complete the chart.

Anne's School Life	Anne... • makes a friendship with _____ • has a _____ with Gilbert • applies for a _____ to a university

Fill in the blanks.

> adopt   orphan   rivalry   mistake   apply for   scholarship

1. I'm sorry I broke your glasses. It was my _____ .

2. Are you going to _____ that job?

3. She became an _____ when her mother and father died.

4. The two teams have a big _____ with each other.

5. Some people _____ children from other families.

6. Peter got a _____ because his grades were very good.

Summary 53

Listen to the summary and fill in the blanks.

Matthew and Marilla _____ Anne, an orphan. She grows up on their farm.

She makes some _____. But she is a good student. She _____ a

_____ scholarship. But Anne has to _____ Marilla after Matthew dies.

Anne gets a _____ job and becomes good friends with Gilbert.

🌀Tip One-Minute Grammar!

Use **want to** to talk about a desire.

They want to adopt an orphan boy.
I want to be a teacher.

A Trip to the Museum

Before You Read

Read and check.

	True	False
1. Students go on field trips.	☐	☐
2. Some museums have dinosaur bones.	☐	☐
3. People watch movies at museums.	☐	☐

New Words

 54

Listen and repeat.

1. **fossil:**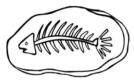

2. **gem:**

3. **subject:** a topic

4. **exhibit:** display

5. **focus:** to concentrate on

6. **semester:** half of a school year

New Sentences

Write a, b, or c.

a 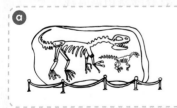　　b 　　c

1. ☐ The museum has fossils of dinosaurs.

2. ☐ The museum has dinosaur exhibits.

3. ☐ The museum has gems like rubies and diamonds.

A Trip to the Museum

• Topic: School Field Trip
• Genre: Nonfiction

Every semester, teachers take their students on trips. They are called field trips. They often visit fun places. They go to zoos or farms. And they often go to museums, too.

Museums have many kinds of exhibits. This way, visitors can learn about all kinds of subjects. Some of them have dinosaur exhibits. So they have old bones and fossils of dinosaurs. These are often very popular. Others have gems like rubies and diamonds.

Some places have other kinds of displays. They may focus on pop culture. They have cars and motorcycles from the past. They also have exhibits from old TV shows, too. So students visiting them can learn about many things.

Listening Quiz! ● 56
1 ⓐ Yes   ⓑ No
2 ⓐ food   ⓑ fossils

Details

Choose or write the answer.

1 Museums have many kinds of _____.

    ⓐ exhibits   ⓑ farms   ⓒ subjects   ⓓ zoos

2 _____ to museums can learn about all kinds of subjects.

    ⓐ Teachers   ⓑ Visitors   ⓒ Dinosaurs   ⓓ Bones

3 What are rubies and diamonds?

    ⓐ statues   ⓑ paintings   ⓒ art   ⓓ gems

4 Where do students often go on field trips?

    - They often go to zoos, farms, and _____.

Main Idea

Choose the main idea.

    ⓐ Students like to go to zoos, farms, and museums.

    ⓑ Some museums have fossils of dinosaurs.

    ⓒ Pop art may be featured at some museums.

    ⓓ Students visit museums on field trips and learn many things.

Organizing

Complete the chart.

Kinds of Museums	Kinds of Exhibits
_____ museum	old bones and _____ of dinosaurs
gem museum	rubies and _____
pop culture museum	cars, _____ , and exhibits from old TV shows

Vocabulary

Fill in the blanks.

> semester exhibit subject fossil gem focus

1 That _____ is worth a lot of money. It's a diamond.

2 There is a special _____ at the museum this weekend.

3 You should _____ on studying when you prepare a test.

4 In Korea, the first _____ of school starts in March.

5 My favorite _____ at school is science.

6 It looks like a _____ of a Tyrannosaurus Rex.

Summary 57

Listen to the summary and fill in the blanks.

Every _____, many students go on field _____ to museums. Museums

have many different _____. So people can _____ about a lot of different

subjects. Some have fossils, and others have _____. Other museums

_____ on pop culture. Some even have exhibits from old TV shows.

> **Tip One-Minute Grammar!**
>
> Use **may** to say that you think something is possible. It can often replace **perhaps**.
>
> Perhaps they focus on pop culture.
> → They **may** focus on pop culture.

Vote for Me!

Before You Read

Read and check.

	True	False
1. Schools have school presidents.	☐	☐
2. A teacher can be the school president.	☐	☐
3. Students study in the cafeteria.	☐	☐

New Words ○ 58

Listen and repeat.

1 clap:

2 vote:

3 collect: to gather

4 improve: to make something better

5 election: choosing by vote

6 run: to be a candidate for

New Sentences

Write a, b, or c.

a    **b**    **c**

1 ☐ We can all collect cans and bottles.

2 ☐ The students clap for Lucy's speech.

3 ☐ The students vote.

Vote for Me!

Grassland Elementary School is having its school presidential election. Only sixth grade students can run. Two students in Mrs. Thagard's class decide to run. They are Lucy and Eric.

Each of them forms a campaign. They tell the students how they will improve the school. Each of them gives a speech to the students. Lucy says, "I will start a school recycling program. We can all collect cans and bottles. Then we can use the money to buy library books." The students clap for Lucy's speech. Then Eric speaks. "We should have free ice cream in the cafeteria every Friday," he says. The students cheer and cheer. Then they vote. It's close, but Eric becomes the new school president.

Listening Quiz! 60

1 ⓐ Yes   ⓑ No
2 ⓐ cans   ⓑ library books

Choose or write the answer.

1. Lucy and Eric each form a _____.

   ⓐ recycling program　ⓑ campaign　ⓒ vote　　　　ⓓ school

2. Eric says they should have free _____ in the cafeteria every Friday.

   ⓐ hamburgers　ⓑ cans　　　　ⓒ ice cream　ⓓ bottles

3. Who will start a school recycling program?

   ⓐ Grassland　　ⓑ Eric　　　　ⓒ Thagard　ⓓ Lucy

4. What grade are Eric and Lucy in?

   - They are in the _____ grade.

Main Idea

Choose the main idea.

   ⓐ Both Eric and Lucy are in Mrs. Thagard's class.

   ⓑ Lucy wants to start a school recycling program.

   ⓒ Eric wins the school presidential election against Lucy.

   ⓓ The students at the school want to have free ice cream.

Organizing

Complete the chart.

Event	Who runs?	Who wins?
school _____ election	_____ and Eric	_____

Fill in the blanks.

> election　　run　　improve　　collect　　clap　　vote

1 My brother likes to _____ both coins and stamps.

2 They always _____ when a player does well in the game.

3 She is going to _____ for Mayor of the city in the next election.

4 You should always _____. It's important in a democracy.

5 The _____ for president will take place tomorrow.

6 I have to _____ my grade in math class.

Summary 61

Listen to the summary and fill in the blanks.

The school is having an _____ for president, so Eric and Lucy both _____.

Lucy says she will start a recycling program to _____ cans and bottles. Eric

wants to give the students _____ ice cream every Friday. It's _____, but

more students _____ for Eric, so he wins.

🔔 Tip　One-Minute Grammar!

My, **your**, **his**, **her**, **its**, **our**, and **their** are possessive adjectives. Use them with a noun to show ownership or possession.

A school is having **its** school election.
My bag is next to **your** books.

After-School Activities

Before You Read

Read and check.

	True	False
1. Some schools have sports teams.	☐	☐
2. Every student does after-school activities.	☐	☐
3. The flute is a musical instrument.	☐	☐

New Words ○ 62

Listen and repeat.

1 **activity**: an action

2 **softball**: a game similar to baseball

3 **join**: to become a member

4 **stay**: to remain in the same place

5 **photography**: picture taking

6 **language**: words that people use to talk and write

New Sentences

Write a, b, or c.

 a

 b

 c

1 ☐ Some students join the photography club.

2 ☐ Some students have language club.

3 ☐ The girls play softball.

After-School Activities

• Topic: School Activities
• Genre: Nonfiction

At most schools in America, classes end at three o'clock. But these days, not every student goes home at three. Instead, many students stay at school. They do many after-school activities.

Many students play sports. Boys usually play basketball and soccer. Girls often play volleyball and softball.

Other students join clubs. There is a club for most subjects. Most schools have math and science clubs. And they also have language clubs. These are often fun for students. Some students join the photography club. They take photos of people and places. And some join the band. Students learn to play the trumpet, flute, clarinet, and other instruments. Then they hold concerts for students and parents.

Listening Quiz! ● 64

1 ⓐ Yes   ⓑ No

2 ⓐ play sports ⓑ hold concerts

Choose or write the answer.

1 Boys usually play _____, and soccer.

    ⓐ basketball   ⓑ volleyball   ⓒ softball   ⓓ tennis

2 Band members learn to play the trumpet, flute, clarinet, and other _____.

    ⓐ photos   ⓑ instruments   ⓒ games   ⓓ clubs

3 What do photography club members do?

    ⓐ speak languages   ⓑ take pictures   ⓒ study math   ⓓ play sports

4 When do most American schools end?

    - They end at _____ o'clock.

Main Idea

Choose the main idea.

    ⓐ Students can play musical instruments in the band.

    ⓑ Sports are very popular activities with students.

    ⓒ It is important for students to do many activities.

    ⓓ Students do many different activities after school.

Organizing

Complete the chart.

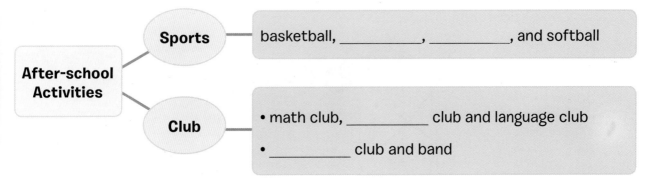

Vocabulary

Fill in the blanks.

> activity   softball   join   language   photography   stay

1. Her favorite _____ is playing computer games.

2. Do you mind if I _____ you and sit down here?

3. He has a nice camera since he really loves _____ .

4. I can only speak one _____ , but Jeff speaks English, German, and Chinese!

5. _____ is my favorite sport to play.

6. Can you _____ here and help me clean my room?

Summary 65

Listen to the summary and fill in the blanks.

After school finishes, many American students do after-school _____. Both

boys and girls play different _____. Other students _____ clubs. There

are clubs for every class. There are also groups like a _____ club. And some

students join a _____ . So they can play musical _____ .

Tip One-Minute Grammar!

Frequency adverbs help us describe how often we do things. They come in before verbs and after be-verbs.

Boys **usually** play basketball and soccer.
She **is always** at the library in the morning.

Vocabulary Index

Vocabulary Index

Develop Reading skills with Vocabulary, Listening, Writing plus Grammar

Reading Plus 2

WORKBOOK

Clue & Key

The Enormous Turnip

A Write the meaning of the word in your mother language. Then write the words.

❶ enormous

❷ entire

❸ grab

❹ purchase

❺ seed

❻ turnip

B Choose the meaning for each underlined word.

❶ He saw an <u>enormous</u> turnip in the garden.

ⓐ very thin   ⓑ very big   ⓒ very small

❷ He <u>purchased</u> some seeds.

ⓐ bought   ⓑ planted   ⓒ ate

C Fill in the blanks.

> grabbed   turnip   entire

❶ He went to the garden and tried pulling the _____ up.

❷ They ate the turnip for an _____ week.

❸ She _____ her husband and pulled together.

D Unscramble the sentences.

1 move / the / didn't / turnip / .

···▶ _____

2 old man / some seeds / purchased / an / .

···▶ _____

3 came / a mouse / and helped / them / .

···▶ _____

4 in / stayed / the turnip / the ground / .

···▶ _____

5 the ground / came / the turnip / out of / !

···▶ _____

E Fill in the blanks. Use the past tense. Grammar

1 His family (move) _____ to another city last year.

2 They (study) _____ math and science at school.

3 I (greet) _____ my friend yesterday.

4 The students (try) _____ to answer the question.

5 She (talk) _____ on the phone last night.

6 We (watch) _____ television this morning.

F Translate each sentence into your mother language.

1 An old man wanted some turnips, so he purchased some seeds.

⋯▶ _____

2 He planted them and went to sleep.

⋯▶ _____

3 The next day, he looked outside. He saw an enormous turnip in the garden.

⋯▶ _____

4 "I'm hungry," he said.

⋯▶ _____

5 He went to the garden and tried pulling the turnip up. It didn't move.

⋯▶ _____

6 "Wife, help me," he called. She grabbed her husband and pulled together, but the turnip didn't move.

⋯▶ _____

7 "Son and daughter, help us," they cried together.

⋯▶ _____

8 His children pulled together, but nothing happened.

⋯▶ _____

9 "Dog and cat, help," said the old man. Everyone pulled together, but the turnip stayed in the ground.

⋯▶ _____

10 Finally, a mouse came and helped them. The turnip came out of the ground!

⋯▶ _____

11 They all ate the turnip for an entire week.

⋯▶ _____

Vegetable Gardens

A Write the meaning of the word in your mother language. Then write the words.

1 common _____ _____

2 produce _____ _____

3 raise _____ _____

4 ripen _____ _____

5 stalk _____ _____

6 vine _____ _____

B Choose the meaning for each underlined word.

1 Some people enjoy <u>raising</u> vegetables in gardens.

   ⓐ growing   ⓑ eating   ⓒ painting

2 Gardens can <u>produce</u> lots of vegetables.

   ⓐ lose   ⓑ move   ⓒ make

C Fill in the blanks.

vines   ripen   stalks

1 Corn grows high in the air on _____.

2 Cucumbers and beans grow on _____.

3 When tomatoes and peppers _____, they change colors.

D Unscramble the sentences.

1 vegetables / there are / kinds of / many / .

…▸ _____

2 shapes / lots of / come in / they / .

…▸ _____

3 under / potatoes / grow / the ground / .

…▸ _____

4 are / good for / they / your health / !

…▸ _____

5 doesn't / corn / underground / grow / .

…▸ _____

E Match to make one sentence. *Grammar*

1 Lots of people visit the beach •

2 Flowers begin to bloom •

3 She likes to go skiing •

4 They visited many countries •

5 The leaves often change colors •

6 The students can get some food •

• ⓐ during her winter vacation.

• ⓑ during lunch.

• ⓒ during the summer.

• ⓓ during the fall.

• ⓔ during their trip.

• ⓕ during the spring.

F Translate each sentence into your mother language.

1 There are many kinds of vegetables. They come in lots of shapes, sizes, and colors.

...▶ _____

2 Some people enjoy raising them in gardens. Cucumbers and beans are often in gardens.

...▶ _____

3 They are both green. And they grow on vines.

...▶ _____

4 Many gardens have tomatoes and peppers. Both start out green.

...▶ _____

5 But when they ripen, they change colors.

...▶ _____

6 Tomatoes turn red, yellow, or orange. And peppers may turn red or yellow.

...▶ _____

7 Potatoes are common. They grow under the ground. So do carrots, turnips, and radishes.

...▶ _____

8 Corn doesn't grow underground. It grows high in the air on stalks.

...▶ _____

9 When it ripens, it turns bright yellow.

...▶ _____

10 During summer, gardens can produce lots of vegetables.

...▶ _____

11 They have many colors. And they are all delicious and good for your health!

...▶ _____

Sally's Flower Garden

A Write the meaning of the word in your mother language. Then write the words.

❶ bloom

❷ bud

❸ dig

❹ dirt

❺ hoe

❻ roots

B Choose the meaning for each underlined word.

❶ I dug up the <u>dirt</u>.

ⓐ plant   ⓑ seed   ⓒ ground

❷ Buds will <u>bloom</u> and have beautiful flowers.

ⓐ blossom   ⓑ grow   ⓒ ripen

C Fill in the blanks.

buds   hoe   roots

❶ I got a _____ and dug up the dirt.

❷ I watered seeds every day to give them strong _____.

❸ My plants are getting bigger and some of them are getting _____.

Ⓓ Unscramble the sentences.

❶ have / they / different / colors / will / .

···▶ _____

❷ my finger / they / as small as / were / .

···▶ _____

❸ I / seeds / planted / some / .

···▶ _____

❹ did / I / what flowers / plant / ?

···▶ _____

❺ it / as high as / a small tree / grow / will / .

···▶ _____

Ⓔ Look at the picture and choose the correct prepositions. Grammar

❶ A girl is (in, on) her flower garden.

❷ The flowers are (above, on) the ground.

❸ There is a rabbit (in, below) the sunflower.

❹ The butterfly is (in, on) the flower.

❺ A girl is standing (below, above) the tree.

❻ There are two birds (above, in) the tree.

F Translate each sentence into your mother language.

1 I'm very excited. Three weeks ago, I started a flower garden in my backyard.

···▶ _____

2 I got a hoe and dug up the dirt. Then I planted some seeds in the ground.

···▶ _____

3 I watered them every day to give them strong roots.

···▶ _____

4 Two weeks ago, they started coming up above the ground.

···▶ _____

5 At first, they were as small as my little finger.

···▶ _____

6 But now my flowers are getting bigger.

···▶ _____

7 Some of them are getting buds. Soon, they will bloom and have beautiful flowers.

···▶ _____

8 Oh, what flowers did I plant?

···▶ _____

9 I planted some irises. And I also have violets and carnations, too.

···▶ _____

10 They will have many different colors.

···▶ _____

11 And I have one sunflower. It will grow as high as a small tree.

···▶ _____

Fruit, Fruit, Fruit!

A Write the meaning of the word in your mother language. Then write the words.

1 arrive

_____

2 field

_____

3 fresh

_____

4 persimmon

_____

5 pick

_____

6 variety

_____

B Choose the meaning for each underlined word.

1 There are many <u>varieties</u> of fruits.

ⓐ shapes　　　　ⓑ kinds　　　　ⓒ times

2 Apples are very popular fruits when fall <u>arrives</u>.

ⓐ produces　　　ⓑ comes　　　　ⓒ ends

C Fill in the blanks.

persimmons　　　fresh　　　pick

1 In spring, grapefruits are _____.

2 _____ are ripe in fall.

3 People _____ strawberries in the fields.

D Unscramble the sentences.

1 persimmons / very popular / fruits / are / .

...▸ _____

2 fruits / can't / many / grow / .

...▸ _____

3 ripe / in summer / peaches / are / .

...▸ _____

4 are / citrus fruits / ripe / like oranges / .

...▸ _____

5 enjoy / strawberries / people / eating / .

...▸ _____

E Make sentences. Use 'so+be+subject.' Grammar

1 Melons are ripe in summer. (so / berries / are) _____

2 They are hungry. (we / so / are) _____

3 The elephant is big. (the / so / hippo / is) _____

4 The pens are small. (pencils / so/ are / the) _____

5 A lion is fast. (cheetah / is / a / so) _____

6 The ring is pretty. (is / so / necklace / the) _____

F Translate each sentence into your mother language.

1 There are many varieties of fruits.

···▶ _____

2 In many countries, fruits grow at different times of the year.

···▶ _____

3 So people can enjoy different fruits all year long.

···▶ _____

4 In spring, strawberries and grapefruits are fresh.

···▶ _____

5 People enjoy eating strawberries as they pick them in the fields.

···▶ _____

6 When summer comes, there are many other fruits.

···▶ _____

7 Cherries, peaches, plums, and apricots are ripe in summer. So are many berries.

···▶ _____

8 Some are blueberries, raspberries, and blackberries. Melons ripen in the summer and fall.

···▶ _____

9 And apples are very popular fruits when fall arrives. So are persimmons.

···▶ _____

10 Grapes and pears are ripe in this season, too.

···▶ _____

11 In winter, it is cold. So many fruits can't grow.

···▶ _____

12 But citrus fruits like oranges and lemons are ripe then.

···▶ _____

Little Red Riding Hood

A Write the meaning of the word in your mother language. Then write the words.

1 gobble _____ _____

2 hood _____ _____

3 lie _____ _____

4 nightgown _____ _____

5 put on _____ _____

6 woodcutter _____ _____

B Choose the meaning for each underlined word.

1 The girl <u>put on</u> her coat and boots.

    (a) hided   (b) wore   (c) bought

2 The wolf ate the grandmother and put on her <u>nightgown</u>.

    (a) nightdress   (b) hood   (c) blouse

C Fill in the blanks.

gobbled   lay   hood

1 The wolf _____ in bed.

2 She gave her granddaughter a riding _____ of red velvet.

3 "I'm a wolf!" the wolf said, and he _____ her up.

D Unscramble the sentences.

1 her / sick / got / grandmother / .

···▶ _____

2 you / strange / look / .

···▶ _____

3 loved / whom everyone / there was / a girl / .

···▶ _____

4 the hood / always / she / wore / .

···▶ _____

5 open / cut / the wolf / he / .

···▶ _____

E Fill in the blanks. Grammar

read	went	saw	slept	ate	came

1 My brother _____ to the supermarket yesterday.

2 We _____ chicken and rice for dinner last night.

3 I _____ a movie with my friend two days ago.

4 Janet _____ that book this morning.

5 Brad _____ home at one o'clock today.

6 She _____ for eight hours last night.

F Translate each sentence into your mother language.

1 There was once a little girl whom everyone loved. Her grandmother especially loved her.

···▶ _____

2 She gave her granddaughter a riding hood of red velvet.

···▶ _____

3 The girl loved the hood, so she always wore it.

···▶ _____

4 Soon, people called her "Little Red Riding Hood."

···▶ _____

5 One day, her grandmother got sick. So she put on her coat and boots.

···▶ _____

6 Then she left home. But a wolf went to her grandmother's house.

···▶ _____

7 He ate the grandmother, put on her nightgown, and lay in bed.

···▶ _____

8 Soon, Little Red Riding Hood arrived. "Grandma, you look strange," she said.

···▶ _____

9 "That's because I'm a wolf!" the wolf said, and he gobbled her up.

···▶ _____

10 Then, a woodcutter came by.

···▶ _____

11 He cut the wolf open, and out came Little Red Riding Hood and her grandmother!

···▶ _____

Teen Clothing Styles

A Write the meaning of the word in your mother language. Then write the words.

1 formal _____ _____

2 hole _____ _____

3 prefer _____ _____

4 resemble _____ _____

5 sweatshirt _____ _____

6 torn _____ _____

B Choose the meaning for each underlined word.

1 Teenagers don't want to <u>resemble</u> their parents.

    ⓐ look like   ⓑ look for   ⓒ look at

2 Teenagers <u>prefer</u> having their own style.

    ⓐ dislike   ⓑ like   ⓒ forget

C Fill in the blanks.

| sweatshirts | formal | holes |

1 The torn jeans have _____ in them.

2 Some teens love wearing _____ and sweatpants.

3 Teenagers often prefer casual clothes to _____ clothes.

D Unscramble the sentences.

1 clothes / some people / formal / like / .

...▶ _____

2 clothing styles / many / there are / types of / .

...▶ _____

3 have / style / their own / teenagers / .

...▶ _____

4 hoodies / love / some teens / wearing / .

...▶ _____

5 dislike / parents / hoodies / teenagers' / .

...▶ _____

E Rewrite the sentences. Use 'prefer.' *Grammar*

1 I like apples better than oranges.

...▶ _____

2 Tom likes pants more than blue jeans.

...▶ _____

3 Susan likes English more than history.

...▶ _____

4 We like rock music more than rap.

...▶ _____

5 They like hiking more than swimming.

...▶ _____

6 The puppy likes bones more than dog food.

...▶ _____

F Translate each sentence into your mother language.

1 There are many types of clothing styles. Everyone has his or her own style.

…▸ _____

2 Some people like formal clothes. Others prefer different kinds of clothes.

…▸ _____

3 Many teenagers have their own style, too.

…▸ _____

4 Teenagers like to look different from other people. They don't want to resemble their pare

…▸ _____

5 They often prefer casual clothes to formal clothes.

…▸ _____

6 Many teens wear T-shirts and blue jeans.

…▸ _____

7 Sometimes, the jeans have holes in them. So people call them torn blue jeans.

…▸ _____

8 Some teens love wearing sweatshirts and sweatpants.

…▸ _____

9 They especially love hoodies. These are sweatshirts with hoods.

…▸ _____

10 However, their parents really dislike hoodies.

…▸ _____

11 They want their children to wear nicer-looking clothes.

…▸ _____

12 But teenagers don't want to do this. They prefer having their own style.

…▸ _____

Catching a Clothes Thief

A Write the meaning of the word in your mother language. Then write the words.

1 clue

_____

2 missing

_____

3 outfit

_____

4 sneak

_____

5 steal

_____

6 thief

_____

B Choose the meaning for each underlined word.

1 The police looked around for <u>clues</u>.

ⓐ items   ⓑ tags   ⓒ hints

2 The thief didn't steal any cheap <u>outfits</u>.

ⓐ furniture   ⓑ shoes   ⓒ clothes

C Fill in the blanks.

| stole   sneaked   missing |

1 The workers found some clothes were _____.

2 The thief _____ into the store.

3 The thief only _____ the most expensive items.

D Unscramble the sentences.

1 the / closed / department store / was / .

···▶ _____

2 clothes / put / in a bag / he / .

···▶ _____

3 doors / opened / the / one of / .

···▶ _____

4 alarm / off / the / went / .

···▶ _____

5 a very / walked into / well-dressed man / the store / .

···▶ _____

E Fill in the blanks. Use the superlatives. Grammar

1 She is the (beautiful) _____ woman in the world.

2 He always reads the (interesting) _____ books.

3 The (formal) _____ men's clothing is the tuxedo.

4 Gold is the (expensive) _____ metal.

5 He gave the (boring) _____ speech yesterday.

6 I think steak is the (delicious) _____ food.

F Translate each sentence into your mother language.

❶ The department store was closed. But, suddenly, one of the doors opened.

····▸ _____

❷ A thief sneaked into the store. He walked all around the store.

····▸ _____

❸ He looked at many different clothes. He saw suits, pants, shirts, and neckties.

····▸ _____

❹ He grabbed many clothes and put them in a bag.

····▸ _____

❺ He didn't steal any cheap outfits. He only took the most expensive items.

····▸ _____

❻ The next day, the workers arrived. They found some clothes were missing.

····▸ _____

❼ So they called the police. The police looked around for clues, but there weren't any.

····▸ _____

❽ Just then, a very well-dressed man walked into the store.

····▸ _____

❾ Beep beep beep! The alarm went off.

····▸ _____

❿ The police grabbed the man. It was the thief!

····▸ _____

⓫ He had forgotten to take the price tags off the clothes!

····▸ _____

Buying Clothes Online

A Write the meaning of the word in your mother language. Then write the words.

1 convenient

_____

2 deliver

_____

3 order

_____

4 return

_____

5 sell

_____

6 try on

_____

B Choose the meaning for each underlined word.

1 Online shopping is easy and <u>convenient</u>.

ⓐ expensive   ⓑ comfortable   ⓒ cheap

2 <u>Returning</u> clothes is inconvenient.

ⓐ Taking after   ⓑ Taking down   ⓒ Taking back

C Fill in the blanks.

order	delivered	try on

1 The clothes will be _____ to their homes.

2 People can't _____ the clothes. So they may buy the wrong sizes.

3 They _____ the clothes by clicking their mouse on the item.

D Unscramble the sentences.

1 go to / website / the company's / they / .

...▶ _____

2 often / people / busy / are / .

...▶ _____

3 to shop / have / they / time / don't / .

...▶ _____

4 are / on / the Internet / they / .

...▶ _____

5 buying / are / many people / clothes / .

...▶ _____

E Fill in the blanks. Use the present continuous. *Grammar*

1 I (eat) _____ a sandwich now.

2 David (watch) _____ a cartoon on TV.

3 They (go) _____ to the park now.

4 Chris and Jay (meet) _____ Jenny now.

5 I (make) _____ a model airplane.

6 Mom (talk) _____ on the phone now.

F Translate each sentence into your mother language.

1 Do you know there are some stores that never close and sell their clothes for 24 hours?

····▶ _____

2 Yes, they are on the Internet.

····▶ _____

3 People are often busy. So they don't have time to shop.

····▶ _____

4 With online clothing stores, they can do their shopping from home.

····▶ _____

5 They just go to the company's website.

····▶ _____

6 Then they find clothes they like and order them by clicking their mouse on the item.

····▶ _____

7 The clothes will be delivered to their homes. It is easy and convenient.

····▶ _____

8 But online shopping isn't perfect.

····▶ _____

9 People can't try on the clothes. So they may buy the wrong sizes.

····▶ _____

10 The real clothes often look different from the ones on the website.

····▶ _____

11 And returning clothes is inconvenient, too.

····▶ _____

12 Still, many people are buying clothes online these days.

····▶ _____

Unit 09 Stone Soup

A Write the meaning of the word in your mother language. Then write the words.

1 drop

2 huge

3 stir

4 taste

5 traveler

6 village

B Choose the meaning for each underlined word.

1 The oldest traveler put a <u>huge</u> pot of water over the fire.

ⓐ very hot   ⓑ very big   ⓒ very tiny

2 Three travelers visited a <u>village</u>.

ⓐ small town   ⓑ small museum   ⓒ small mountain

C Fill in the blanks.

> tasted   travelers   dropped

1 The traveler stirred the soup and _____ it.

2 The oldest traveler _____ a big stone in the pot.

3 The _____ were hungry, but no one gave them any food.

D Unscramble the sentences.

1 fire / the traveler / a / started / .

···▶ _____

2 are / what / you / making / ?

···▶ _____

3 by all / the soup / enjoyed / was / .

···▶ _____

4 gave / them / no one / any food / .

···▶ _____

5 is / the most / this soup / delicious / .

···▶ _____

E Combine the two sentences. Use 'but.' Grammar

1 Jason likes math. He is not good at it.

···▶ _____

2 She has a pet dog. She prefers cats to dogs.

···▶ _____

3 I'm tired. I have to do my homework now.

···▶ _____

4 Lisa studied hard. She got a bad grade.

···▶ _____

5 She watched the movie. The movie was boring.

···▶ _____

F Translate each sentence into your mother language.

1 Three travelers visited a village.

···▶ _____

2 They were hungry, but no one gave them any food.

···▶ _____

3 The oldest traveler started a fire and put a huge pot of water over it.

···▶ _____

4 Then he dropped a big stone in it.

···▶ _____

5 "What are you making?" asked a villager. "Stone soup," he answered.

···▶ _____

6 "Stone soup? What's that?" he asked.

···▶ _____

7 "It's delicious, but it needs carrots to have a better flavor," the traveler said.

···▶ _____

8 The villager ran to his house and brought some carrots back.

···▶ _____

9 The traveler stirred the soup and tasted it.

···▶ _____

10 "Not bad, but it could use some potatoes," he said.

···▶ _____

11 Another villager put in some potatoes. Soon, every villager put something in the soup.

···▶ _____

12 "This is the most delicious soup ever," said someone. The soup was enjoyed by all.

···▶ _____

Pots and Pans

A Write the meaning of the word in your mother language. Then write the words.

1 equipment _____

2 flat _____

3 fry _____

4 liquid _____

5 roast _____

6 stew _____

B Choose the meaning for each underlined word.

1 Every cook needs some <u>equipment</u> in the kitchen.

    ⓐ outfits   ⓑ food   ⓒ tools

2 It's a <u>flat</u> pan perfect for making pancakes.

    ⓐ even   ⓑ hard   ⓒ thin

C Fill in the blanks.

liquids   roast   fry

1 Cooks _____ chickens in the oven.

2 They are able to _____ eggs on the frying fans.

3 These pots can hold lots of water and other _____.

D Unscramble the sentences.

1 cooks / have / most of / many pots / .

···▶ _____

2 some cooks / stew / make / in the pots / .

···▶ _____

3 like / big pots / some cooks / having / .

···▶ _____

4 are / too / roasting pans / helpful, / .

···▶ _____

5 wouldn't / cook / they / able to / be / .

···▶ _____

E Rewrite the sentences. Use 'be able to.' Grammar

1 A chef can cook well.

···▶ _____

2 My brother can ride a bicycle.

···▶ _____

3 Eric can speak Korean.

···▶ _____

4 The cat can catch mice.

···▶ _____

5 He can play baseball well.

···▶ _____

6 I can read books quickly.

···▶ _____

F Translate each sentence into your mother language.

1 Every cook needs some equipment in the kitchen.

...▶ _____

2 So, most of them have many pots and pans.

...▶ _____

3 Without them, they wouldn't be able to cook.

...▶ _____

4 Some cooks like having big pots. They make stew and soup in them.

...▶ _____

5 And they also cook pasta like spaghetti in them.

...▶ _____

6 These pots can hold lots of water and other liquids.

...▶ _____

7 Cooks use smaller pots for making sauces.

...▶ _____

8 Cooks always have many kinds of pans, too. They especially need frying pans.

...▶ _____

9 They are able to fry eggs, hamburgers, and other kinds of food on them.

...▶ _____

10 Roasting pans are helpful, too.

...▶ _____

11 Cooks put chickens or hams on them and then roast them in the oven.

...▶ _____

12 Finally, most cooks have a griddle. It's a flat pan perfect for making pancakes!

...▶ _____

Unit 11

Sara's Cookies

A Write the meaning of the word in your mother language. Then write the words.

1 burn _____ _____

2 flour _____ _____

3 horrible _____ _____

4 ingredient _____ _____

5 lump _____ _____

6 tray _____ _____

B Choose the meaning for each underlined word.

1 I put <u>lumps</u> of cookie dough on a tray.

    ⓐ pieces   ⓑ cups   ⓒ kinds

2 The cookies looked <u>horrible</u>!

    ⓐ wonderful   ⓑ terrible   ⓒ delicious

C Fill in the blanks.

> burning   ingredients   tray

1 I smelled something _____.

2 I put the _____ in the oven.

3 I got all the _____: flour, sugar, eggs, butter, and chocolate chips.

D Unscramble the sentences.

1 really / looked / good / it / .

···▶ _____

2 let's / some / buy / cookies / .

···▶ _____

3 for / we / twenty minutes / talked / .

···▶ _____

4 what / mom / great / a / !

···▶ _____

5 won't / what happened / believe / you / .

···▶ _____

E Unscramble the sentences. Use 'What a ~!' Grammar

1 an / book / what / interesting / ! ···▶ _____

2 what / cake / delicious / a / ! ···▶ _____

3 fun / what / game / a / ! ···▶ _____

4 boring / a / game / what / ! ···▶ _____

5 a / what / story / sad / ! ···▶ _____

6 elephant / what / big / a / ! ···▶ _____

F Translate each sentence into your mother language.

1 I tried making some cookies yesterday. You won't believe what happened.

...▶ _____

2 First, I got all the ingredients. I needed flour, sugar, eggs, butter, and chocolate chips.

...▶ _____

3 I mixed everything together. It looked really good.

...▶ _____

4 Then I heated the oven. I put lumps of cookie dough on a tray.

...▶ _____

5 And then I put it in the oven. But guess what happened next?

...▶ _____

6 My friend Amy called me. We talked for twenty minutes.

...▶ _____

7 Then I smelled something burning. It was the cookies!

...▶ _____

8 They looked horrible! Then my mother came home.

...▶ _____

9 She went to the kitchen and looked at me and my cookies.

...▶ _____

10 And then she said, "Let's go to the store and buy some cookies."

...▶ _____

11 What a great mom!

...▶ _____

A Special Restaurant

A Write the meaning of the word in your mother language. Then write the words.

1 castle _____ _____

2 cheer _____ _____

3 customer _____ _____

4 feast _____ _____

5 knight _____ _____

6 unique _____ _____

B Choose the meaning for each underlined word.

1 They eat a delicious <u>feast</u> of meat and vegetables.

ⓐ snack   ⓑ dinner   ⓒ entertainment

2 Theme restaurants make dining a <u>unique</u> experience.

ⓐ usual   ⓑ common   ⓒ special

C Fill in the blanks.

| castle   cheers   customers |

1 Every diner _____ for the knights.

2 The restaurant looks like a _____.

3 _____ get a wonderful meal and entertainment.

D Unscramble the sentences.

1 ride / knights / horses / the / .

⋯▶ _____

2 a / look like / it / restaurant / doesn't / .

⋯▶ _____

3 you / the 15th century / in / are back / !

⋯▶ _____

4 fight / other / each / they / .

⋯▶ _____

5 the show / knights / there are / in / six / .

⋯▶ _____

E Rewrite the sentences. Use 'look like.' Grammar

1 Steve resembles Trevor.　　　⋯▶ _____

2 The picture resembles a painting. ⋯▶ _____

3 The pen resembles a pencil. ⋯▶ _____

4 The magnet resembles a coin. ⋯▶ _____

5 That bird resembles a penguin. ⋯▶ _____

6 My sister resembles my mother. ⋯▶ _____

F Translate each sentence into your mother language.

1 As you walk down the stairs, you can see the gothic dining room.

····▶ _____

2 Now, you are back in the 15th century!

····▶ _____

3 Theme restaurants make dining a unique experience.

····▶ _____

4 One of them is Medieval Times.

····▶ _____

5 It doesn't look like a restaurant. It looks like a castle!

····▶ _____

6 Diners go back to the Middle Ages at this place.

····▶ _____

7 They get to eat a delicious feast of meat and vegetables.

····▶ _____

8 But that's not the best part. There is a show at the restaurant.

····▶ _____

9 There are six knights in the show. Every diner cheers for the knights.

····▶ _____

10 The knights ride horses. They fight each other for over two hours.

····▶ _____

11 So customers get a wonderful meal and entertainment during their night out.

····▶ _____

Anne of Green Gables

A Write the meaning of the word in your mother language. Then write the words.

1 adopt

_____

2 apply for

_____

3 mistake

_____

4 orphan

_____

5 rivalry

_____

6 scholarship

_____

B Choose the meaning for each underlined word.

1 Anne makes many <u>mistakes</u>.

   ⓐ friends   ⓑ jobs   ⓒ errors

2 She <u>applies for</u> a scholarship.

   ⓐ sends   ⓑ gets   ⓒ requests

C Fill in the blanks.

| adopt | scholarship | rivalry |

1 Matthew and Marilla want to _____ an orphan boy.

2 Anne has a _____ with Gilbert.

3 Anne gets a _____ to a university.

D Unscramble the sentences.

1 becomes / an excellent / Anne / student / .

...▶ _____

2 on / a farm / Matthew and Marilla / live / .

...▶ _____

3 Diana / with / makes / a friendship / she / .

...▶ _____

4 to stay / home / decides / Anne / .

...▶ _____

5 Gilbert and Anne / friends / close / become / .

...▶ _____

E Unscramble the sentences. **Grammar**

1 want / I / a / book / read / to / .   ...▶ _____

2 movie / to / they / a / watch / want / .   ...▶ _____

3 he / his / homework / do / wants / to / .   ...▶ _____

4 here / wants / stay / to / Nancy / .   ...▶ _____

5 to / to / I / sleep / want / go / .   ...▶ _____

6 want / dinner / have / they / to / .   ...▶ _____

F Translate each sentence into your mother language.

1 Matthew and Marilla live on a farm called Green Gables.

···▶ _____

2 They want to adopt an orphan boy to help on the farm.

···▶ _____

3 But the orphanage wrongly sends a girl, Anne.

···▶ _____

4 At first, Anne makes many mistakes. But she still tries very hard.

···▶ _____

5 At school, she makes a friendship with Diana but has a rivalry with Gilbert.

···▶ _____

6 As Anne grows up, she becomes an excellent student.

···▶ _____

7 She applies for a scholarship to a university, and she gets it.

···▶ _____

8 However, Matthew suddenly dies of a heart attack.

···▶ _____

9 And Marilla has some health problems. Anne decides to stay home.

···▶ _____

10 Gilbert gives his teaching job to Anne.

···▶ _____

11 So she can stay close to home and care for Marilla.

···▶ _____

12 After Gilbert does this, he and Anne become close friends.

···▶ _____

A Trip to the Museum

A Write the meaning of the word in your mother language. Then write the words.

1 exhibit   _____   _____

2 focus   _____   _____

3 fossil   _____   _____

4 gem   _____   _____

5 semester   _____   _____

6 subject   _____   _____

B Choose the meaning for each underlined word.

1 Visitors can learn about all kinds of <u>subjects</u>.

     ⓐ problems   ⓑ topics   ⓒ shows

2 Museums have many kinds of <u>exhibits</u>.

     ⓐ displays   ⓑ farms   ⓒ movies

C Fill in the blanks.

gems	semester	focus

1 Every _____, teachers take their students on trips.

2 Some exhibits _____ on pop culture.

3 Some museums have _____ like rubies and diamonds.

D Unscramble the sentences.

1 are / called / they / field trips / .

...▶ _____

2 fossils / have / they / of dinosaurs / .

...▶ _____

3 often / are / these / popular / very / .

...▶ _____

4 go / they / to / museums / often / .

...▶ _____

5 many things / about / can / students / learn / .

...▶ _____

E Rewrite the sentences. Use 'may.' Grammar

1 Perhaps Jane is at home.

...▶ _____

2 Perhaps the dog likes bones.

...▶ _____

3 Perhaps she is in the bath.

...▶ _____

4 Perhaps he is a teacher.

...▶ _____

5 Perhaps she takes many classes.

...▶ _____

6 Perhaps they go cycling.

...▶ _____

F Translate each sentence into your mother language.

1 Every semester, teachers take their students on trips. They are called field trips.

···▶ _____

2 They often visit fun places. They go to zoos or farms.

···▶ _____

3 And they often go to museums, too.

···▶ _____

4 Museums have many kinds of exhibits.

···▶ _____

5 This way, visitors can learn about all kinds of subjects.

···▶ _____

6 Some of them have dinosaur exhibits.

···▶ _____

7 So they have old bones and fossils of dinosaurs. These are often very popular.

···▶ _____

8 Others have gems like rubies and diamonds.

···▶ _____

9 Some places have other kinds of displays. They may focus on pop culture.

···▶ _____

10 They have cars and motorcycles from the past.

···▶ _____

11 They also have exhibits from old TV shows, too.

···▶ _____

12 So students visiting them can learn about many things.

···▶ _____

Vote for Me!

A Write the meaning of the word in your mother language. Then write the words.

1 clap _____ _____

2 collect _____ _____

3 election _____ _____

4 improve _____ _____

5 run _____ _____

6 vote _____ _____

B Choose the meaning for each underlined word.

1 Lucy and Eric will <u>improve</u> the school.

ⓐ recycle ⓑ visit ⓒ upgrade

2 We can <u>collect</u> cans and bottles.

ⓐ drink ⓑ gather ⓒ buy

C Fill in the blanks.

clap	election	run

1 The school is having its presidential _____.

2 The students _____ for Lucy's speech.

3 Two students decide to _____ for election.

D Unscramble the sentences.

1 a campaign / them / forms / each of / .

⋯▸ _____

2 to / run / two students / decide / .

⋯▸ _____

3 the / cheer / students / and vote / .

⋯▸ _____

4 they / a speech / the students / to / give / .

⋯▸ _____

5 becomes / Eric / school president / the new / .

⋯▸ _____

E Fill in the blanks with the correct possessive adjective. Grammar

1 That is Eric's book. It is _____ book.

2 Susan has some hairpins. They are _____ hairpins.

3 Tom and I have some pencils. These are _____ pencils.

4 I am wearing glasses. They are _____ glasses.

5 We have a clock. That is _____ clock.

6 You are holding a notebook. That is _____ notebook.

F Translate each sentence into your mother language.

1 Grassland Elementary School is having its school presidential election.

　…▸ _____

2 Only sixth grade students can run.

　…▸ _____

3 Two students in Mrs. Thagard's class decide to run. They are Lucy and Eric.

　…▸ _____

4 Each of them forms a campaign. They tell the students how they will improve the school.

　…▸ _____

5 Each of them gives a speech to the students.

　…▸ _____

6 Lucy says, "I will start a school recycling program. We can all collect cans and bottles. Then we can use the money to buy library books."

　…▸ _____

　　 _____

7 The students clap for Lucy's speech.

　…▸ _____

8 Then Eric speaks. "We should have free ice cream in the cafeteria every Friday," he says.

　…▸ _____

9 The students cheer and cheer. Then they vote.

　…▸ _____

10 It's close, but Eric becomes the new school president.

　…▸ _____

After-School Activities

A Write the meaning of the word in your mother language. Then write the words.

1 activity

2 join

3 language

4 photography

5 softball

6 stay

B Choose the meaning for each underlined word.

1 Students do many after-school <u>activities</u>.

ⓐ actions   ⓑ homework   ⓒ sports

2 Many students <u>stay</u> at school.

ⓐ learn   ⓑ play   ⓒ remain

C Fill in the blanks.

join   softball   photography

1 They join the _____ club. They take photos of people.

2 Some students _____ the language club.

3 Girls often play volleyball and _____.

D Unscramble the sentences.

1 usually / boys / soccer / play / .

...▶ _____

2 at / end / three o'clock / classes / .

...▶ _____

3 most subjects / a club / there is / for / .

...▶ _____

4 students and parents / they / concerts / hold / for / .

...▶ _____

5 learn / the trumpet / to play / students / .

...▶ _____

E Answer the questions. Use frequency adverbs. *Grammar*

1 How often do you study English?

(always)_____

2 How often is John late for class?

(never)_____

3 How often do they go to the library?

(often) _____

4 How often does she meet her friends?

(sometimes) _____

5 How often is she happy?

(always) _____

6 How often are you awake at midnight?

(usually) _____

F Translate each sentence into your mother language.

1 At most schools in America, classes end at three o'clock.

···▶ _____

2 But these days, not every student goes home at three.

···▶ _____

3 Instead, many students stay at school. They do many after-school activities.

···▶ _____

4 Many students play sports. Boys usually play basketball and soccer.

···▶ _____

5 Girls often play volleyball and softball.

···▶ _____

6 Other students join clubs. There is a club for most subjects.

···▶ _____

7 Most schools have math and science clubs. And they also have language clubs.

···▶ _____

8 These are often fun for students.

···▶ _____

9 Some students join the photography club. They take photos of people and places.

···▶ _____

10 And some join the band.

···▶ _____

11 Students learn to play the trumpet, flute, clarinet, and other instruments.

···▶ _____

12 Then they hold concerts for students and parents.

···▶ _____

Reading Plus

Reading Plus is a three-level reading series that helps elementary-level learners develop their reading skills. It provides various types of reading genres and a huge variety of topics. The systematic activities such as the warm-up questions, listening quizzes, and grammar tips help students expand and upgrade their English level.

Features

- Various types of genres: classic tales, fiction stories, and nonfiction articles
- High-interest topics appealing to elementary school students in higher grades
- Warm-up questions that help students build comprehension and understand new words
- A variety of reading activities including Listening and Grammar activities
- Workbook: reviews of words and sentences, translations, etc.

Components

Student Book / Workbook / Audio CD

Downloadable Resources: **http://www.clueandkey.com**